Storm Run

By Libby Riddles
Illustrated by Shannon Cartwright

Storm Run

ISBN 0-934007-31-4
Library of Congress #96-71195
Paws IV Publishing
P.O. Box 2364
Homer, Alaska 99603
Copyright Libby Riddles ©1996
Illustrations copyright Shannon Cartwright © 1996
All rights reserved
First edition 1996
Library of Congress Cataloging in Publication Data
Riddles, Libby-The true story of the first woman to win the 1100 mile Iditarod
Sled Dog Race after challenging a killer storm off the coast of Alaska.
Printed on recycled paper

To my mom and dad
Thanks for always believing in me.
L.R.

The arctic blizzard ripped across the tundra. The Eskimos probably had a word for such a storm. Something that meant "wind-driven snow that cuts and freezes bare skin." It was a cold that could kill.

A raven riding the wind dipped toward a spot of color on the ice below. The young woman struggled with the frozen zipper on her sled bag, trying to escape the brutal wind. It hammered her, howling savagely down from the north like a wounded animal. Sky and sea ice dissolved into a world of churning snow. Her huskies were already buried comfortably beneath the drift. Human beings really had no business out in such weather.

She knew she might freeze to death tonight, or go on to become the first woman to win the Iditarod Sled Dog Race. Right now she was too tired and cold to care which.

I grew up in the Midwest. As a child I spent endless days reading books about animals. The woods surrounding our house were magic, with treasures of hidden flowers, odd mushrooms and rotting wood that glowed in the dark. There were berries to eat, creeks to wade and trees to climb. Winters were full of skiing, fast and fun, with the glorious smell of the mountain air.

By the age of five, I'd figured out my life ambition. I was going to be a rancher and have as many animals as I wanted. I was already doing a good job of improvising, with a stick horse named Lightning, a cowgirl outfit and a way of bringing home any kind of critter who wandered into my path. It was this little girl's dream that eventually led me north to the Iditarod Trail.

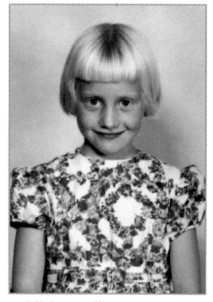

Libby at five years old

ALASKA.

In the name, I heard the whisper of wilderness calling. It was 1973 and as a gawky 16 year old living in St. Cloud, Minnesota, I was sick of cities and ready for a new life. I worked hard all winter, saving money from a day job and finished my last two years of high school in six months of night school. Then I followed my dream.

ALASKA.

My parents were concerned. I was still young and it was so far away. But once they saw how determined I was they supported my decision. Along with my four sisters and two brothers, my family saw me off at the airport.

Friends from Minnesota got me started in Alaska. I was totally green when I showed up in an old secondhand beaver coat and high-heeled sheepskin boots. I had no idea how to fend for myself. It was scary but exciting too. I just had faith that things would turn out. I settled near Nelchina and learned to live Bush style: building a cabin; burning wood for heat; carrying water from a mountain stream and eating moose meat.

One winter day during a grocery run to Anchorage, I ended up in the the crowd of the 1973 World Championship Sled Dog Race. Ssswish! I watched as the teams of huskies flew around corners then disappeared in the distance, all legs and quiet speed, scattering the sparkling snow. In that moment, I fell in love. Dog driving was the most exciting and beautiful thing I'd ever seen. The part of me that always felt close to nature began to sing.

I was determined to build my own sled-dog team. Husky rejects soon surrounded the cabin. If someone had tried to sell me a three-legged dog I probably would have bought it.

They were a motley gang. Not one was a leader. When I tried to run them they fought and chewed the lines.

After breaking up the fights I sat on the sled and cried. I wondered if I would ever be a musher. It sure wasn't as easy as it looked. But I kept at it. I made the dogs haul firewood and water for me and finally they started to behave.

In my cabin at night, I'd pull the chair close to the stove, turn the kerosene lamp up high and read about polar explorers. I shivered as I read of Shackleton and Byrd, trudging for thousands of frozen miles, driven to be the first to accomplish an extraordinary feat. Then I'd blow out the lamp and snuggle down into my cozy sleeping bag, extra glad for the warmth.

R ick McConnell, an Iditarod musher, startled me one day by telling me I should run a race. I thought anyone who ran the long distance races was crazy. I was happy just to have the dogs for company and help with the wood and water hauling. But he had a short five mile race in mind. What was there to lose? I hooked up my best dogs and astounded myself by winning the race! "Gee, racing might not be so bad after all!"

The next thing I knew, I was planning to run the Iditarod.

There was so much to do! I talked to other mushers and read whatever I could about training and caring for dogs. My friends helped out when they could.

The plan was to spend the winter of 1979 training like we were running the race, but wait until the next winter to run it. I didn't kid myself about how much experience I needed to finish a thousand-mile marathon.

I worked hard. My chores taught me the meaning of endurance. It didn't matter if the weather was bad or I was not feeling good. The dogs needed care, no matter what. Every day I lugged steamy buckets of food and water to the dogs, and shoveled the yard. I bucked up deadwood with a chainsaw and hauled it down the hill on an indestructible 2x6 sled. I hauled "people" water three miles from Nelchina Lodge in five-gallon cans and melted snow for the dogs in buckets balanced around the stove. I sewed dog booties and nylon collars. I was always hungry. Often I'd return home so starved from the long miles on the trail that I'd snack the dogs quickly, then run to the cabin for a bite of food so I'd have the juice to unharness the team.

I signed up to run the 180-mile Cantwell-Denali Highway Race, to get a taste of what was ahead. Afterward I went over all the mistakes I'd made. Solo, a spooky, no sense of humor leader I bought from Iditarod champion Rick Swenson, was the biggest surprise. Before the race, the lean, hard-bodied husky had not been very cooperative, but as soon as we hit the trail, he was Mr. Business.

I ran my first Iditarod in 1980, when trail conditions were bad. As a rookie, I was too dumb to know it was worse than normal, so I kept plugging away and came in 18th place out of 60 teams, the second rookie to finish.

The race had been very hard and I'd been cold and tired. Still, there was something special about the way the

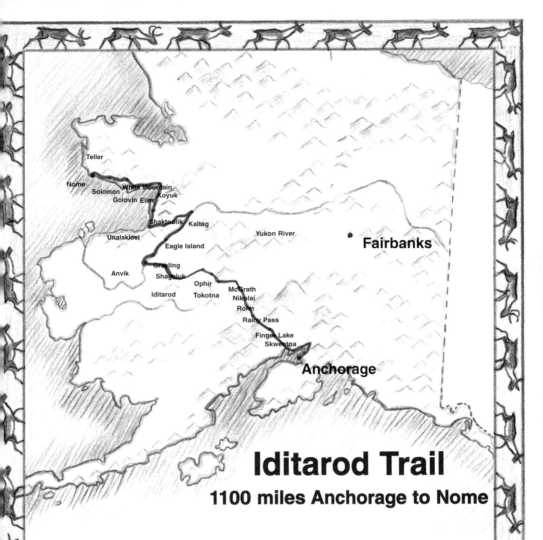

Teller

Nome
Solomon · White Mountain
Golovin Elim · Koyuk

Shaktoolik · Kaltag
Unalakleet
Eagle Island · Yukon River · **Fairbanks**

Anvik · Grayling
Shageluk
Ophir · McGrath
Iditarod · Tokotna · Nikolai
Rohn
Rainy Pass
Finger Lake
Skwentna

Anchorage

Iditarod Trail
1100 miles Anchorage to Nome

Iditarod challenged me to be and do my very best. I liked that. And I loved spending all that time with my dogs.

My education continued. I raced again the next year, full of awe at how extreme conditions could be up on the arctic coast and amazed at the native people who had somehow thrived there.

I didn't know how it would work out, but I was going to move to the Arctic. Heading north with a planeload of dogs, I'd send for Danger, my cat, when I got settled in.

I ended up in the small coastal Eskimo village of Teller, north of Nome, working together with Iditarod musher Joe Garnie, who grew up there. We'd met on the Iditarod Trail. The pups bred from my first Iditarod team were raised in Teller, and I hoped they would grow up to be my new Iditarod stars.

Joe and I fished for the dogs. In the short summers, cut salmon glistened richly as it dried on the fish-camp racks.

In the fall, wearing our warmest clothes, we fished at night pulling hundreds of pounds of sparkling, sweet smelling herring to shore in our beach seine. Even in the winter we fished, with nets strung through holes in the ice, pulling out Northern Pike and fat whitefish which were pulled back to camp by the dogs. Sometimes I'd get pretty sore, but I didn't let it stop me.

Axle, Sister and Dugan

T he pups grew up following the big dogs on training runs. One slender brown pup would always be ahead of the team, leading the way. Every once in a while, he would stop and wait impatiently for the rest to catch up. His name was Dugan.

Dugan's brother, Axle, was like a baby-sitter to Sister's pups. Sister was Joe's leader and she wanted to get back in the team and wasn't interested in taking care of pups at all. So Axle stayed behind and huddled under the porch, licking and caring for Sister's litter.

By the start of the 1985 Iditarod, the young dogs were four years old, and had grown into tough, lanky huskies. They'd been tested on the Kusko 300 Race and Joe had raced a combination of our young dogs to a third place finish in the 1984 Iditarod. Not too shabby for their first time out.

People in Teller saw me out in the dog yard every day taking care of my team. They watched from warm, cozy houses as I harnessed up, determined to train in the bitter weather. When no one else would help sponsor an unknown musher like me, the people of Teller pitched in with their bingo money.

On the morning of March 2, 1985, the teams stretched out at the Iditarod starting line on Fourth Avenue in downtown Anchorage. I gripped the handlebar as the announcer counted down the time. It was hard not to be nervous. The dogs were barking and going berserk.

Four brothers made up the heart of my team: Shy, furry Binga; Bug-man, who had a broken toe as a pup and was now a great leader; Axle, the well-mannered one; and Dugan, the super-star leader. My first Iditarod leader, Solo, was grandfather to the twins, Minnow and Tip. Lively young Inca barked and yipped to go.

The oldest dog on the team was Joe's shaggy but savvy leader, Sister. She was mean and she was ugly but there wasn't one ounce of quit in her. Sister's pups, Stripe and Whitey, ran in the middle. Fat, red Dusty was Joe's leader, but didn't like to lead for me. Socks, Brownie, Stewpot, and sweet Penny rounded out the rest of my 16-dog team.

"Three, two, one!" the race announcer shouted, and we were off. Traveling through Anchorage with a fresh team was so dangerous, we got to bring another person to help control the sled until we reached Eagle River. Joe was riding a second sled behind mine when we had our first disaster. The dogs took a short-cut through the woods, bouncing the sled off trees and crashing through alders.

"Hang on!" I yelled as we went airborne over an old half-buried washing machine. The pull of the dogs kept me upright, but Joe crashed in a heap, crunching his arm. I spent most of that afternoon jamming my brake as we careened around boulders and through metal culverts.

Running under the stars that night, exhausted, I was thankful that I always seemed to have such good bad luck. The metal brake on my sled finally snapped outside of Knik, but I'd been able to find a replacement before leaving civilization. Later that afternoon, I'd stopped to give the dogs a snack, but they weren't ready to rest, and they snapped the tree they were tied to like a twig.

The first rule of dog mushing is NEVER LET GO OF YOUR SLED. If you do let go, the only thing that will stop the dogs is if the sled or hook accidentally gets caught on something. I grabbed wildly for the snub rope, dragging face down in the snow for as long as I could before my hands gave out. For a moment, I lay there, not believing my team was disappearing down the trail, and my hopes for the race were going right along with them. Then I bolted after them, screaming and hollering for them to stop, just in case they'd listen.

Good luck came in the form of Chuck Schaeffer, another musher who caught up from behind and offered me a lift, and a second

Checkpoint at Rainy Pass

musher, Terry Adkins, who managed to stop and tie up my wayward dog team farther up the trail. None of the dogs were hurt, and I was grateful that the Iditarod was the kind of race it was; mushers often helped each other out.

The snow was really deep in 1985, which meant moose were a problem. It made sense that the gigantic animals would rather walk on the packed trail than flounder in deep snow.

The hard to reach buds they munched on and the tough traveling made the moose cranky.

Several mushers had run-ins with them, including Susan Butcher, who had two of her dogs killed before another racer shot the moose. My team came up on one moose, but Lavon Barve had already snowshoed a trail around the stubborn animal and I wisely took the detour.

As the miles fell away the pressure began to build. Joe had done well with this same team the year before. Would I be able to do as well? "Don't worry about it," I told myself, "Just do the best you can, that's all you can do."

As the teams drew closer to the mountains of the Alaska Range the weather got worse. At Rainy Pass, we got the bad news. The pass was closed. The pilots hadn't been able to get dog food to the checkpoints beyond. On Day 3, the race was 'frozen' for 70 hours. We had to stay put until the pilots could make it through. People from Anchorage donated dog food to be shipped out for our teams. I stretched out the food I had as long as I could. Every couple of hours, I'd melt snow in the cooker and add a little meat to make broth. I found spruce branches and made little beds for the dogs to sleep on.

Up at Rainy Pass Lodge, I found an empty bunk. The only problem was one of the other mushers snored so loud I couldn't sleep. The noise was making me crazy, so I reached down where I'd seen some pillows. I was going to throw one at the guy, but instead of a pillow, my hand latched on to the face of another sleeping musher! I wasn't sure which one of us was more scared. Someone finally shook the snoring guy, and he quieted down before the whole cabin collapsed.

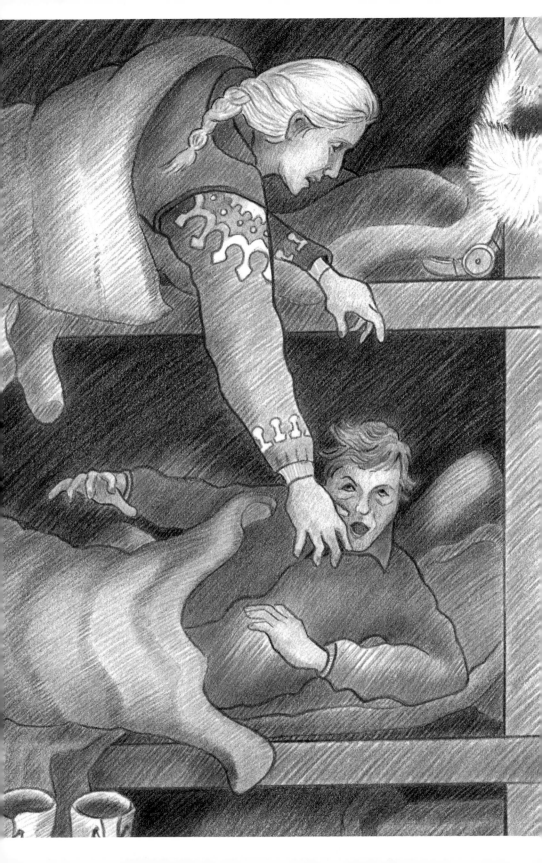

In the morning, the race began again, the teams making it across the Pass and over the Farewell Burn to Alaska's Interior. Things were going okay until the weather once again shut the race down at the Ophir checkpoint. It was a day and a half before we could leave.

On Day 11 we reached the Yukon, the biggest river in Alaska. got colder and colder as the wind raged from bank to bank, erasing any trail. In the last faint wash of a fading red sunset I saw a fire winking in the darkness ahead. Two mushers were thawing out and, since it was time for a break anyway, I stopped to snack the huskies and try to get warm.

It was hard prying myself away from the comforting fire, but was soon back on the trail with a chilly night stretched ahead. Before long, we came to a lodge with several sleds pulled up in front. The lights and the smell of food tugged at me but I had just rested the dogs. It sure was tempting though. While I was trying to decide, the dogs were trying to pull me up to the lodge. I didn want them to get bad habits after I'd worked so hard to train them, so up the Yukon we went.

Ve moved into the blackest of nights. I couldn't make out any
unner tracks. In fact, I could barely see the trail. I was either lost,
r in first place.

It was 40 below at Eagle Island when I finally reached the
heckpoint and found out I was in the lead.

The next night on the way to Kaltag, the bottom dropped out.
Vith the sun sinking in a cold gold ball the temperature also
lummeted. Around here they call that kind of weather 'severe
lear.'

It was 60 below, so cold I had to pull out my sleeping bag and
vear it around me like a cape to keep even a little warm. I ran or
edaled constantly to keep my feet from freezing in the damp
hoepacs. During that spooky, dangerous night I cursed the cold
ke it was some primitive, mad animal. The dogs pulled steadily,
he frost of their breath making them look like ghost dogs. The
veather didn't seem to bother them at all.

Dugan had been running lead almost all the way. I tried other
ogs up front with him, and was surprised that Axle, who had
ever led before, seemed to do the best.

It seemed to me that he did it because he had a great big heart, and wanted to help however he could. As the northern lights flickered coldly overhead, I thought of how proud I was of these dogs I'd raised from pups, and how much I loved them all. They didn't know about winning, they just knew they had a job to do and they did it eagerly.

At first light I headed out of Unalakleet before anyone else. My dogs seemed happy to reach the coast; maybe they could tell they were closer to home. I had to leave Stripe behind, because his feet were a little sore. The checkers would take care of him and ship him by plane to Nome.

As we climbed the hills on the way to Shaktoolik, a storm was picking up. By the time we hit the flats, it was blowing snow in our faces, and I stopped to put on warmer clothes. A big crowd turned out in the bad weather to welcome me. I knew a lot of the people in the village, and had worked there for a while when I first moved north. They were excited that I was in front!

I had some hard decisions to make in the hours ahead. I knew how dangerous these storms could be, but I didn't want the other mushers to catch me when I'd worked so hard to get ahead. If they did, everyone would wait until the weather got better, then sprint on to Nome and the faster teams would get me.

But was it worth risking my life for? I was scared, but I had worked too hard, for too many years, to let a blizzard stop me. I fed the dogs, and while they rested I ate with friends. From inside, the weather looked even worse.

I called Joe in Nome from the
he would say that even if it
watched myself, not quite belie
into the storm. I collected my dry
his head in disbelief. This made me
The dogs seemed to think that
it. If anyone was the weak link in
the snow off and we started out of
"This is CRAZY!" I kept sayir
war in my head. I could hardly
I argued. I was going to do wh
into the Bering Sea the tempera
Fear made me careful. I felt
couldn't see from one marke
us without losing sight (
north wind, until I fo
crawled across
through a bo

ne in town, and he told me to get out there, get going, but I knew
 below and a tornado. I was the one who had to decide. In a daze, I
ny own feet took me around in the snow, getting ready to head out
 booted up all 56 paws. Another musher pulled in, and he shook
tle stubborn, and helped to keep my feet moving.
 willing to go, so were they. I never doubted that they could make
n, it was me. I pulled the hook. "Okay gang. Let's go." They shook
ige.
self over and over as we drove into the swirling snow. It was like a
thing, everything was white and moving. "This is a RACE!"
mised myself in the beginning; the best I could. As the sun dipped
bed with it. Fifty, maybe sixty below with the wind chill factor.
unted animal; there was no relief from the relentless weather. I
next, so we'd travel as far as we could from the marker behind
n I'd hook down the team and walk ahead, fighting the gusting
next marker. Then I'd go back for the dogs. Inch by inch we
ice. The visibility was about like it would be if you were wading
y powder except this white stuff had sharp, cutting edges.

The dogs keyed in on the intensity of the situation. Despite the wind that screamed in their ears and the ice that froze on their fur, they were game as long as I was. We trusted each other. They could have turned around and bolted back to Shaktoolik while I looked for markers up ahead, but they didn't. They curled up as only northern animals can do, and patiently waited for me.

It was slow going, but death lurked on either side of the trail. Open water, hypothermia: so I stayed focused. One marker, then another. I was already pushing my luck. My clothes were getting wet from the inside out as I battled for every step. I'd learned the hard way on several other trips how miserable it felt to start getting chilled in damp clothes, how easily the heat seeped out. For now I was warm and running on pure adrenaline. Fortunately, I still had a few pieces of dry clothing in the sled. Whether I could get into them without freezing my hands was still to be seen.

Battling the storm on sea ice

One thing was certain. I wasn't turning back. Each step was too hard won. I tackled the blizzard like some summit-crazed mountaineer.

Once we were on the sea ice, losing the markers could mean stumbling through bad ice and ending up with a quick trip to the Happy Hunting Grounds. No, I wasn't ready to die yet.

As daylight faded, it became even harder to see. The risk of getting lost grew worse. I realized that I wasn't going to be so lucky as to have the lights of Koyuk guide me across to the checkpoint. There would be a break in the battle. I was shutting down for the night.

I stopped the sled next to a trail marker and fought for a while with the frozen sled bag zipper. A raven sped by on the wind above us. It was the only other creature crazy enough to be out in this weather. I found the bag of snacks and gave each dog several pieces. By the time I'd emptied the sled, they were curled in weather-proof circles.

The sled bag was small, but big enough to get away from the wind. It was such a relief. For a moment I lay on my back and the darkness spun like black snow. There I was, in a deadly arctic blizzard, protected by a thin nylon skin, warmed by the knowledge that I'd survived.

Then I started to get cold.

The fun wasn't over yet. I knew I'd have to change into my dry clothes somehow without freezing my fingers. If I stayed in the wet clothes, hypothermia would find me. There was no choice.

The sled bag was much smaller than a tent, so changing clothes inside it was out of the question. I'd unzip the bag, perform one step of my clothing routine,

then scoot back into shelter to thaw out my hands before performing the next step. It took a couple of hours to get situated and into my sleeping bag, but it was mighty cozy when I did. I slept mindlessly, switching from side to side on the hard basket slats.

When I woke up on the 16th day of the race, it was getting light. I was shamelessly warm in my bag and had no intentions of going anywhere soon. I drifted back into oblivion. I woke up, suddenly realizing that if I didn't get up and get going, I could be having to spend ANOTHER night out on the ice. I had no dry clothes for back-up and now my sleeping bag was probably damp as well.

I searched around inside the bag for the gloves I'd stashed for drying. Then I got my arms out so I could reach the zipper of the sled bag. For a panicky moment, the zipper refused to budge, frozen shut. Then I ripped it open. The cold bit into me as I peeked out.

I noticed I was talking to myself again, walking myself through the steps, keeping myself calm.

"Okay, where are the gloves? Find the gloves."

"That's good. Now the first thing you do when you're up is hop into your mukluks."

"Do you have them ready? Good. Okay, open the zipper and go!" I managed to slip into the mukluks without the wind knocking me down.

The storm wasn't close to blowing itself out yet. It was as bad or worse than the day before. I couldn't see the next marker, but there was still one right there next to the sled, waiting patiently like an old friend.

The dogs were so buried, I wasn't sure which lumps were them. I called them up, "Hey huskies! Up we go!"

They popped up out of their snowy beds like grouse. They yawned and stretched. I went to each dog, petting the ice off of them. I gave each one a snack of lamb. Their double coat of fur kept the cold out. They were rested and ready to go. I wasn't hungry, but I made myself eat some Norwegian chocolate and chased it with seal oil; Eskimo power food. Then we hit the trail.

Once we were moving, it was a real struggle to keep from freezing my face. I couldn't look for markers with goggles on. I strained to find each new marker, but my eyes grew raw as I wiped first one, then the other, with my mittened hand. My Native-style fur ruff protected my face as I took turns looking with first one eye and then another. Back at Shaktoolik, the other mushers were more worried about me being hurt than having me beat them. They sat inside until late morning, drinking coffee and eating hotcakes and hoping the weather would get better, but it didn't. Outside the storm hammered the walls and wailed through the stovepipes. Snow pelted the windows and doors looking for any crack. No one wanted to go out, but it was still a race. A few of them finally headed out into the wind around 11 a.m. By then, I had been on the trail for a couple of hours. My friends around the state worried, hoping that I could pull it off.

I n Nome, Joe told them to wait before they sent out search and rescue, that I could handle it, that I wouldn't turn back.

Traveling in the storm was still incredibly difficult. If we ever did get across to the other side, I was going to kiss the snow bank. In an effort to keep my parka dry, I'd pulled my rain poncho on, belting it down with a rubber bungee cord. Then I stuffed polar fleece dog booties next to my face to keep it from freezing. Another handful of booties filled the gaps in the hood that the wind tried to find.

Time went by slowly. Dugan put his nose down and muscled straight into the wind. He remembered the trail from last year and knew Nome was out there somewhere. I put other dogs in lead, trying to give him a rest. Dusty led reluctantly, with his tug line slack, but it was worth it for a while as he seemed to have a knack for following the markers. But I ended up having to put Dugan back in before long. It would have been tough going without him. We were making pretty good progress when all of a sudden, there were no more markers and the ice looked new and green and dangerous.

Quick! What to do? Maybe Sister will know. I switched her to lead and hoped for the best. Half-way across the bad ice, I started to think Sister was taking us too far off course, and I yelled over the wind at her, "Gee! Sister, gee!" trying to get her to go to the right. But Sister had her own plan and kept stubbornly pulling us off to the left. The sled couldn't have stopped on the ice, so I held on and let them go. Then, like a mirage, a trail marker appeared! Sister had found the trail! We were back on the safe ice and I hooked down and ran up to

give Sister a big fat hug and a kiss on her scarred face.
"Good Girl! You're SOOOOO smart! Good job!"

The village of Koyuk was just ahead. Never had any
sight looked sweeter. Snowmachines were already on
their way out to meet us. "We did it! We really did it!" I
said to the dogs. My friend Vira came and gave me a big
hug.

Everyone was asking me questions, but mostly I just
wanted to get my dogs bedded down and fed. I gave them

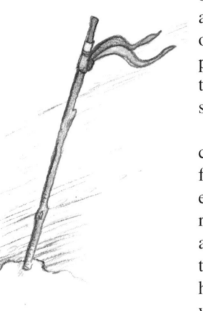

beds of straw, a warm meal
and everyone a thorough going
over. Luckily, we were a bit
protected from the storm, with
the village being on a
south-facing hill.

Inside Vira's house I
couldn't believe how good it
felt to be out of the wind. My
ears still hummed with the
roar of it and my face was hot
and wind-burned. I covered
the house with wet clothes,
hanging them wherever there
was room. A few hours later,
after a short sleep and the little I could eat of the huge
turkey dinner Vira had made, I looked out the window
across the ice and still couldn't see the headlights of any
mushers following me. I hoped they hadn't gotten lost. It
was still storming, but it was time for me to go.

The wind wasn't quite as bad. We traveled cross-wise
to it now, west towards Elim. I had hot cakes with bacon
grease on top at my friends', Fritz and Bessie's, and

decided I would drop Sister here. It was so hard to leave behind a member of the team, but Sister had a little bit of frostbite on her belly so it would be safer to leave her with the checker. "We'll see you in Nome, sweetie," I said, scratching her neck. "Thanks for all the help."

Up "Little McKinley," down to Golovin, over to White Mountain. I was so tired it was all a blur. In the checkpoint, I fed my dogs as they rested in the afternoon sun. A veterinarian checked the dogs and told me what I

already knew: they looked great. Joe and some friends surprised me by showing up. I was glad to see them, but it seemed weird. I was still racing and not ready to relax. A short nap just made me sleepier, but we drove down the river and were soon in the Topkok hills.

Once we were out of the hills on the lagoon, the wind picked up. Several times I got blown right over, dragging until I could get the dogs to stop. They looked back at me, impatiently wondering what the delay was. They seemed to have picked up speed, like they knew we were getting close to the end.

Somehow in the dark we took a wrong trail. It was two in the morning, but a light was on in one of the few cabins. I knocked on the door. "Where am I?" I asked the old Eskimo whose eyes twinkled when he saw who stood on his porch. "Don't worry, those guys won't catch you! You're in Solomon, just go right over there and it will take you to the Safety checkpoint." So, turning around with my headlight batteries almost gone, I started out again. After a few miles, I noticed something funny. I was looking at sled dog tracks. I was the only team out there, so it didn't take too long to figure out I had gotten turned around and was following my own trail and going back the way we had come! It's so easy to make mistakes when a person is tired.

It seemed like it took forever to get to the Safety checkpoint. I knew those other mushers were several hours behind me, so I had some soup and lay down for awhile before heading out on the final stretch to Nome.

The sun was just coming up over the Bering Sea when we left the checkpoint. The dogs were pulling strong, Axle and Dugan leading the team. The Arctic was so beautiful and this was the best way to see it. I was sad that soon it would be over. I switched on my radio just in time to catch Hobo Jim's Iditarod Trail song. He was singing, "There are no sled tracks in front of me and no one on my tail, I did, I did, I did the Iditarod trail."

It felt like the song had been written just for me, for that exact place and time. The tears froze on my face as I finally let myself believe that we were actually going to win this race. Not even a tidal wave or an earthquake could knock us out of first place now.

Closer to Nome, people started coming out on snowmachines, taking pictures, waving and smiling. I waved back. The dogs were excited too, and started to run. I was so proud of them, I thought my heart would burst.

There was the finish line, and hundreds and hundreds of people, all cheering for us. I had done my best, and even surprised myself.

Sister was watching the race on T.V. at the checker's house in Elim. The announcer asked me what it felt like to win. Without thinking, I said, "What it feels like, is if I die now, it'll be okay."

Of course I didn't die then, and I'm still having adventures with my dogs, living a life I'd dreamed up when I was a kid.